Accounting and Finance
for
Non-finance Professionals.

Help is on the way!

Claude Phiri

ISBN-978-1-724-40557-9 (Amazon.com) Claude Phiri

Dedication

To all those professionals that find themselves lacking when it comes to accounting and finance. This book is dedicated to you as you make effort to acquire knowledge and skills in the fundamental concepts in accounting and finance.

Contents

	Page
Preface	v
Acknowledgements	vi
1. Introduction	1
2. The quad model	8
3. Financial statements	28
4. Time value of money	38
5. Capital budgeting techniques	47
6. Analysis and interpretation of financial statements	55

Preface

Do you get the chills when it comes to numbers and figures? Do you always wonder what on earth they're talking about when they present those financial statements? Have you found yourself thrust into a management role that requires you to have to deal with them numbers and you have no clue where to start? You are so good at what you do and a great professional in your field of specialisation but feel so lost when it comes to managing and reporting on finances related to your unit or department. Well, you are in the right place. Help is on the way. In fact, help is here. In this book, I take a selection of some accounting and/or finance concepts that you are likely to meet every so often and explain them in such a way that you may never forget after you have learnt them. In the book, I use the same style and techniques that I have used with thousands of students and other learners over the years and put this to pen and paper for your benefit, too. I have helped many pass their exams and others get to grips with these concepts I am confident you will find help too. Help is here for you.

Claude Phiri

Johannesburg

July 2018

Acknowledgements

I wish to pay tribute to the many students and course participants that I have had the privilege to teach or tutor and from whom I have learnt and refined some of the methods of communicating these accounting concepts in such a way that makes it easy to understand. Students that we have been our clients at Mapalo Tuition Centre, some learners at Regenesys Business School and the scores of short course participants that I have trained over the years.

You all have not only been my students, you have helped develop me as a teacher and trainer too. Working with you has helped sharpen the way that I communicate the messages to make them easily   understood.

Chapter 1

INTRODUCTION

In this chapter, we will introduce both financial accounting and financial management, before moving on to discuss other topics in the two study areas.

What is accounting?

Accounting could be regarded as a language. A language that is used to convey financial information about an entity (company or any other type of organisation for that matter).

Accounting conveys information relating to an entity's financial position and financial performance. We will return to this a little later.

Just like any other language has rules and guidelines that govern its usage, accounting in the sense of being a language also has rules and guidelines on how to use it in order to convey the desired information.

It behoves both the sender and the receiver of the accounting information so conveyed to have an understanding of the language in order to attach meaning to what is being said. Hence the need for you to understand some of the basic tenets of the language of accounting and hence, this book, among others.

Why accounting?

Accounting is used as a means to convey information in order to help the users to make informed decisions regarding the entity.

Accounting also provides a system by which an entity can and must keep records of its accounting transactions in order to extract reports or summaries at the end of the period. Reports that provide the financial information that, in turn, aids the various users' decision-making.

Users of accounting information

We can classify users of the financial information that an entity provides into two categories; internal and external users.

Internal users of the financial information are those within the entity and include management and employees. Management will be interested to know how the entity is performing and its financial position to help them manage better. Employees may be interested in the financial information of the entity to see if their jobs are secure and sometimes to determine how much to bargain for in terms of an increase in emoluments for example. They would want to know if the employer can afford a particular demand for instance.

External users do not form the internal class of users but have an interest in the goings on of the entity. They include investors or would be investors who will want to determine if the entity is worth placing their money in. Lenders, like banks or other finance houses that need some form of assurances that the entity will be able to pay back any borrowed funds. Suppliers of goods or services on credit also have a similar motive for wanting to know the financial information of the entity. They want to know that the entity will be able to pay for the goods or services that are supplied on credit.

Other external users include government agencies such as tax authorities that want to know what the profits of the entity were in order to determine how much tax to levy the particular entity.

Branches of accounting

The demarcation of the two main branches of accounting is related to the discussion we have just had (above) on the two main categories of users of financial information that the entity provides.

Management accounting

Financial information that is provided to internal users is usually in the form of management accounts. Management accounts will have specific details that are relevant to the nature of business and the information needs of the management of the particular entity. To a large extent, management accounts are not prescribed. An entity may have management accounts prepared and presented in a format that is not necessarily the same as another entity.

For instance, an entity that manufactures motor vehicles may require different details such as door panels and wind shields and so on. Information on these will help management of the motor manufacturer to manage their entity better. Whereas the management of, say a hospital facility may need details about bed occupancy and information on consumption of drugs and the like.

The branch of accounting that focusses on information for decision making by internal users is within the domain of management accounting. This also includes information on budgets, costing or forecasts that are used in managing the entity better.

Financial accounting

Financial accounting information is primarily addressed to users who are external to the entity. One of the main differences between the two branches of accounting is that financial accounting is highly prescribed. The format, the details and the rules that govern how these are maintained and the reports generated from such records are prescribed. Communicating in the language of financial accounting is the same everywhere, regulated by international standards and in some countries, by legislation. A debit in one country is a debit in every other country for example. The format of the financial statements is similar across the globe.

We will return to the financial statements that are prepared and presented for external users later.

Underlying assumption (Going concern)
Whenever accounts for an entity are prepared, they are prepared with the assumption that the entity will continue existing and doing business in the foreseeable future. Otherwise the numbers in the financial statements may have to be amended if this were not the case.

An example will help demonstrate the importance of this concept. Let us assume the business owns a $100,000 truck that has been in use for the last two years. If the policy of the entity is to depreciate straight line at 20%, at the end of the second year, the vehicle will have depreciated by 40% (20% in the first year and another 20% in the second). Depreciated at the end of the second year will be $40,000. In the books of this entity, the value of the vehicle will now be at $60,000 (100,000-40,000).

Now let's say that the vehicle has done a lot of mileage and on very rough terrain to the extent that it is impossible to fetch even half the $60,000 value if the entity were to sell it. Without making any adjustments in the records of the entity, the $60,000 value of the vehicle would be overstated as it would clearly be worth much less.

The going concern principle assumes that the entity will continue in business as usual so that the vehicle will be reported at the $60,000 value in the books of the entity. And yet the real forced resale value is probably only $30,000. The value of $60,000 would have to be reduced to the $30,000 if it was known that the entity was shutting down in, say two months from the reporting date. This would be done in order to reflect a more accurate record of the value of the truck in the books of the entity.

International Financial Reporting Standards (IFRS)

IFRSs represent internationally accepted accounting practices that most, if not all, countries and entities adopt or adapt as the case may be. One major aim is to bring about global uniformity in the field and practice of accounting.

Various IFRSs and the predecessor International Accounting Standards (IASs) are developed to address different aspects of accounting.

We will not go into any further detail on this one. Now let us briefly discuss financial management.

What is financial management?

Finance can be defined as the art and science of managing money. Virtually all individuals and organisations earn or raise money and spend or invest money.

Finance is concerned with the process, institutions, markets and instruments involved in the transfer of money among individuals, businesses and governments.

The goal of the firm

- *Maximise profit?*

Some people believe that the firm's objective is always to maximise profit. Companies commonly measure profits in terms of earnings per share.

But is profit maximisation a reasonable goal? NO. This goal ignores the timing of returns, cash flows to shareholders and risk. We will revisit the idea of timing of cash flows in a later chapter.

- *Maximise shareholders' wealth*

The goal of the firm, and therefore of all managers and employees, is to maximise the wealth of the owners for whom it is being operated. The wealth of corporate owners is measured by the price of the shares, which in turn is based on the timing of returns, their magnitude and their risk. Because share price represents the owners' wealth in the firm, maximising share price will maximise owner wealth.

Why study managerial finance?

An understanding of the concepts, techniques and practices of financial management will acquaint you with the financial manager's activities and decisions. Because most business decisions are measured in financial terms, the financial manager plays a key role in the operation of the firm.

People in all areas of responsibility need a basic understanding of the managerial finance function.

All managers in the firm, regardless of their job descriptions, work with financial personnel to justify labour requirements, negotiate operating budgets, deal with financial performance appraisals and sell proposals at least partly on the basis of their financial merits. Those managers who understand the financial decision-making process will be better able to address financial concerns and will therefore more often get the resources they need to attain their own goals.

The principles covered in this book apply to all types of organisations, profit-seeking firms and not-for-profit organisations. The decision-making principles can also be applied to personal financial decisions

Chapter 2

The Quad Model

(Simple Way to Understand Balance Sheet, the Income Statement, the Accounting Equation and the Duality Principle using one diagram)

Let's now introduce the quad model that I have used many times to help explain the two key financial statements, the Balance Sheet (Statement of Financial Position) and the Income Statement (Statement of Profit or Loss and Other Comprehensive Income). Don't stress, we will not go all technical jargon on you. I mention them here so we are sure you do not get lost when these terms are used elsewhere, at your work for instance.

What are financial statements?

Simply put, financial statements are the collection of four specific financial reports that are prepared in respect of an entity to show both the financial position and performance of that entity. We will explain each of these reports or statements in a later chapter.

Elements of financial statements

First let us start with the elements or building blocks that we will use to create our model. In accounting, any event that happens is called a transaction. So when you buy something, it is a transaction. You sell something, transaction; you transfer inventory from one place to another, transaction; you borrow from the bank, a transaction. There are hundreds or even thousands of transactions that take place on a regular basis, depending on what you do. Accounting has found a way of breaking these transactions into five categories depending on their nature. At the end of the day, each one of the many transactions must be classified and placed

into one of these five categories called elements. A transaction can only be in one category and no other.

From whose perspective?

All the transactions that take place are recorded from the perspective of the business. So if you make a sale, it is recorded from the angle of you having made the sale and NOT from the perspective of the buyer.

There is a distinction between the owner of the business and the business itself. For example, if the owner of a business takes money out of his own pocket and invests it into the business, the accounting record will be made in the books of the business as having received the money from the owner. We will come back to this thought shortly. For now, let us be satisfied that we record all accounting transactions from the perspective of the business.

The Quad Model

I use this term quad derived from the full word quadrant because the model I am about to show you has four (quad) squares that make up the model.

First we draw four quadrants into which we will be slotting content as I explain.

Step 1 – draw four squares on a sheet of paper, like below;

Step 2 – Start placing transactions into the appropriate square.

Earlier, we alluded to the 5 elements that are the building blocks of financial statements. We didn't give them names yet. We will do so here.

So as transactions take place, they are classified and grouped into one of the elements or building blocks we have talked about and then placed into one of the four squares in the quad model. Eventually, all the transactions that are similar in nature will end up in the same square in the model. Put differently, each of these squares are like home to one of the elements of the financial statements.

Let's start with the top left one. It's important that we place these labels on the correct square, otherwise the model will not work, it may confuse us instead.

Assets In this square, we will place any transaction that meets the criteria of being called an asset. What is an asset, you ask? Simply put, an asset is anything that the business owns. If your business owns the building that your offices are in, the value of the building is recorded as an asset in the books of your company. If you own a motor vehicle, that is also an asset to the business.

Also, if someone owes the business something, that also is an asset because it is yours even though you may not have possession of it at the moment.

Assets may be long term or short term in nature. This distinction and definition is prescribed by international standards.

Non-current assets
Assets from which you will derive benefit for a period longer than the current financial year (or 12 months) are called non-current assets. Examples include buildings, motor vehicles, plant and machinery, furniture and fittings as well as equipment.

Current assets
Current assets refer to those that your business will derive benefit from within the current financial year (12 months period). Examples include inventory that you assume will sell within the current financial year, any balances of those who owe you and are likely to pay with the current financial year and the balance in your account at the bank.

Now, let us place this type of transactions in their appropriate home in the quad model.

Assets • What you own or what you have a claim/right over like the balance of what someone else owes your business. • Could be non-current asset (long term) or current asset (short term)	

Next we check for transactions that will go into the top right square. Two types of transactions make this square their home, so to speak. First liabilities and then equity or capital.

Liabilities

A liability is the balance of what your business owes someone else. Like assets, liabilities may be long term (non-current liabilities) or short term (current liabilities).

Non-current liabilities are those that your business will continue to pay back over a period longer than the current financial year. Examples include a long term loan from the bank, a mortgage loan or debentures.

On the other hand, **current liabilities** are those that your business is likely to pay back within the current financial year. These include your bank overdraft or the unpaid balances you owe for the supply of inventory that you bought on credit.

One more type of transaction also makes their home in the same square, and that is Equity.

Equity
Equity represents the investment by the owner into the business. By nature, it is as if the business owes this to the owner so it sits in the same home as liabilities that the business owes to other people. Remember we are looking at all these records from the perspective of the business, and not necessarily the owner of the business.

Ok, now let us place these transactions in their home on the model:

Assets	Liabilities
• What you own or what you have a claim/right over like the balance of what someone else owes your business. • Could be non-current asset (long term) or current asset (short term)	• What you owe. • Could be non-current liabilities (long term) or current liabilities (short term) **Equity** • The investment or capital that the owner has put into the business.

So far so good? Great.

Let's now take a look at transactions that fall into the bottom two squares, starting with income.

Income

A record of the money that came into the business as a result of what you do. If you sell products, money that came in as a result of your selling transactions is income. If you sell services, the fees that others pay you for your services is income.

I would like us to talk about the last type of transactions before we place both of them into their respective homes in the model.

Expenses

This is money spent in order to earn the income you have recorded above. For example, your purchases of inventory (if you sell groceries) that you sold or expenses relating to the maintenance of the store (rent, lights, water, salaries, etc.). These would be classified as expenses.

Accruals

We must clarify that it does not matter if cash has been paid for your inventory or whether you sold on credit and have not yet received the cash from the sale. The transaction must be recorded and reported when it takes place and not when the cash is received or paid. So the total income should include sales of things for which you are still expecting to receive the cash. Your expenses, likewise, must include those that you have incurred but not yet paid for.

Ok, now we are ready to send these two types of transactions to their respective homes in the quad model.

Assets	Liabilities
Assets • What you own or what you have a claim/right over like the balance of what someone else owes your business. • Could be non-current asset (long term) or current asset (short term)	**Liabilities** • What you owe. • Could be non-current liabilities (long term) or current liabilities (short term) • **Equity** The investment or capital that the owner has put into the business.
Expenses • Money going out, spent on what we needed to have done for us to make the income that we made.	**Income** • Money coming in from what we do as a business.

Back to the elements of financial statements Can you see the five elements that are the building blocks of financial statements? In the quad model, it's the five that are in bold. ALICE, someone has said. I actually do not know who to give credit to for this one but it is an easier way to remember the five elements of financial statements using this acronym, ALICE. The A stands for assets. The L stands for Liabilities. The I represents income. The C is for capital and the last E stands for expenses. Five of them. Got it? You're doing well.

Armed with this understanding, I will now take the quad model a little further and show you how the balance sheet and the income statement feature in the model.

Balance Sheet

Assets	Liabilities
• What you own or what you have a claim/right over like the balance of what someone else owes your business. • Could be non-current asset (long term) or current asset (short term)	• What you owe. • Could be non-current liabilities (long term) or current liabilities (short term) • **Equity** The investment or capital that the owner has put into the business.
Expenses • Money going out, spent on what we needed to have done for us to make the income that we made.	**Income** • Money coming in from what we do as a business.

Income Statement

Next, please draw a line across, in between the top two and the bottom two squares as shown in the diagram above.

You have two top squares that are homes to three of the five elements of financial statements: Assets, Liabilities and Equity (Capital).

The balance sheet
If you were to list the balances of the three elements in the top two Squares in the quad model, you would have for yourself a balance

sheet, now formally called the Statement of Financial Position. The balance sheet lists all the assets, liabilities and equity with their respective values. It is intended to show you the true value or worth of the business at any given time.

The balance sheet of a big conglomerate may look complicated and may contain so much information but the bottom line is that it shows a list of the totals of the three elements. What does the business own (assets), what does the business owe (liabilities) and what is the difference between them (equity), which is the true worth or value of the business.

The next time you come across the financials of your company or organization, take a closer look. You will notice that there is a statement of financial position or the balance sheet. That statement shows a summary of the total values of the assets and liabilities that the entity has. The difference between the two shows the true worth (equity) of that entity.

It's like looking at your own financial position at any given time. If we take the total value of what you own and subtract the total of everything you owe, we can determine how much you are worth (your equity). That is how Forbes and other organisations determine how rich Patrice Motsepe, Bill Gates, Richard Branson or someone else.

Now take a look at the bottom two squares of the model. On the left, you have expenses and income on the right. The difference between the aggregate totals of these two gives you either a profit or a loss, depending on whichever one is the higher of the two.

A summary of these two squares gives rise to the Income Statement. (or more fully, the Statement of Profit or Loss and Other Comprehensive Income).

So far, we have been able to determine the statement of financial position and the statement of income by using the quad model. Makes it easier, right? I think so too.

Debit or credit?

One more point before we move on to the accounting equation, which is also related to the quad model.

In the books of your business, how do you know which of the elements is supposed to go to the debit or to the credit side of the ledger?

Draw a line in between the squares on the left and those on the right hand side of the model as shown in the diagram.

Assets	Liabilities
• What you own or what you have a claim/right over like the balance of what someone else owes your business. • Could be non-current asset (long term) or current asset (short term)	• What you owe. • Could be non-current liabilities (long term) or current liabilities (short term) • **Equity** The investment or capital that the owner has put into the business.
Expenses	Income
• Money going out, spent on what we needed to have done for us to make the income that we made.	• Money coming in from what we do as a business.

- **Debits**

The two elements on the left hand side of the model (assets and expenses) will all have a debit balance. In other words, they will increase on the debit side of the ledger.

- **Credits**

The three elements on the right hand side will have a credit balance, increasing on the credit side of the ledger.

The Basic Accounting Equation or The Accounting Equation

Another concept that we can explain using the quad model is called the accounting equation. The accounting equation says that the total of all assets is equal to the sum of all the liabilities and equity. Assets = Liabilities + Equity.

Let's reproduce the model to help us once again. This time we will only look at the top two squares of the model.

Assets	Liabilities
• What you own or what you have a claim/right over like the balance of what someone else owes your business. • Could be non-current asset (long term) or current asset (short term)	• What you owe. • Could be non-current liabilities (long term) or current liabilities (short term) • **Equity** The investment or capital that the owner has put into the business.

Have you noticed that the assets of the business will have been bought using the two sources of financing a business; borrowings (liabilities) and equity. What happens is that you take the capital and turn it in to the business, it becomes an asset, as far as the business is concerned. You borrow from a bank for example or from a supplier, and this translates into an asset to the business. At the end of the day, the total of all the liabilities and the equity must equal the total of the assets that the business has.

An example will help make this clearer.

Let's say you take $1,000 of your own money to put into the business as capital. This will go into the right hand square as equity or capital, right? At the same time, the business will record an asset of $1,000 in the form of cash received from you.

Assets		Liabilities	
Cash or bank	$1,000		$0
		Plus	
		Equity	$1,000

After recording this transaction, you see how that the assets value is equal to the value of the liabilities and equity square, put together. This principle will remain true in every case, as long as we have recorded the transaction correctly in terms of the classification into the five elements of financial statements is concerned.

Duality principle Also referred to as double entry, the duality principle posits that every transaction has a dual effect. For example, when you make a sale, there is also a buyer at the same time. Similarly, any debit entry will always attract a credit entry and vice versa.

Here is an example;

You decide to buy equipment worth $2,500, on credit, from a store in town called EquipSuccess.

In your records, you will enter $2,500 on the debit side of your ledger because you will be recognizing an asset that your business has just acquired. On the other hand, you will have to recognize the debt of $2,500 as a result of the one and same transaction, the dual effect.

Continuing with the quad model, this is how it appears now;

Assets		Liabilities	
Cash or bank	$1,000		$2,500
Equipment	$2,500	Plus	
		Equity	
		Capital	$1,000
Total	$3,500	Total	$3,500

A combination of the liabilities with equity is equal to the total of the two assets that this business has. The duality principle remains true and the accounting equation also remains in balance after every transaction.

The General ledger

In accounting speak, the general ledger (GL), is the collection of all the smaller subsidiary or subledgers into which you record the debit and credit transactions of a business. These subledgers are classified into the five elements referred to above.

Some of them represent assets, others liabilities and so on. So when a transaction takes place, we must first determine which two of the five elements are affected and then decide how to record the same.

The golden rule is that every debit entry must have a corresponding credit entry, again the duality principle must always be satisfied when recording any accounting transaction.

An example will do, but now showing the ledger entries as they would appear in the books of the business. Let's take the two transactions that we used as examples earlier.

First, there was the example of the owner putting a $1,000 into the business and then the business buying $2,500 worth of equipment on credit.

Assets		Liabilities	
Cash or bank	$1,000		$2,500
Equipment	$2,500	Plus	
		Equity	
		Capital	$1,000
Total	$3,500	Total	$3,500

Using the ledger or T-accounts as they are sometimes referred to;

We will debit the asset accounts and then credit the capital and liability accounts, in our general ledger (GL) as we saw earlier. The left hand side of the ledger is the debit and the right, credit, respectively.

Bank Account (an asset account in our GL)

1 000	

Equipment (an asset account in our GL)

2 500	

Capital (equity account in our GL)

	1 000

EquipSuccess (a liability account in our GL)

	2 500

Closing off ledger accounts Each subsidiary ledger account needs to be closed at the end of every period, usually monthly in order to establish the closing balance. This closing balance is then transferred (closed off) to the Trial Balance (TB) where all the balances are collected, debit balances to the debit and credit balances to the credit. I will not go into the process of closing off ledger accounts. Suffice to say that the closing balance is transferred to the TB.

The Trial Balance (TB)

As indicated in the paragraph above, the trial balance is a collection of the ending or closing balances from all the subledger accounts that a business has. The debit balances are posted to the debit of the TB while credit balances are posted to the credit of the TB.

Now, if the debit entry of every transaction has had a corresponding and equal credit entry, you would expect that the two sides of the TB, debit and credit, will be equal. That is one of the main reasons for compiling the TB; to indicate to you, on face value at least, if you have posted all the debits and credits correctly.

In the TB, all your assets and expenses will be on the debit side while all your liabilities and equity will be on the credit side. This satisfies the accounting equation too.

Using the information from our earlier examples, the trial balance will look like shown below;

Trial Balance

Bank	1 000	Capital	1 000
Equipment	2 500	Liability	2 500
Total	**3 500**	**Total**	**3 500**

The trial balance serves as the source of information in order to compile the financial statements (balance sheet and the income statement).

At this stage, and since we haven't had any sale in the business in our example, the Balance sheet would simply show what we have on the date of reporting as follows;

Company Name
Statement of Financial Position as at 30th June 2018

Assets

Non-current assets

Equipment	2 500
Current assets	
Cash and cash equivalents	1 000
Total assets	3 500

Equity and liabilities

Capital	1 000
Non-current liability	2 500
Current liabilities	-
Total assets	3 500

Referring back to the quad model, you notice that all three of these elements of financial statements (assets, liabilities and equity) are taken from the top two squares of the model. The accounting equation is held true as you may have noticed; Assets (3,500) = Liabilities (2,500) + Equity (1,000).

Chapter 3

FINANCIAL STATEMENTS

A set of financial statements for an entity refers to the four financial reports that are produced to show the financial position and performance in respect of the reporting period, be it a quarter or a year as well as some notes to the accounts and accounting policies of the entity.

We will now discuss each of the four statements and the accompanying accounting policies and notes to the accounts.

Statement of financial position

You were introduced to the statement of financial position in the discussion on the quad model in chapter 2. It is one of the reports that are prepared primarily for external users of an entity's financial information. It is drawn to show the total values of the assets, liabilities and equity at a particular point in time. It's format is prescribed by international standards.

Even though it is always listed first in the financial reports that entities present, it is not necessarily the first to be prepared. The profit or loss is the first of the four to be prepared. The profit or loss calculated is carried forward as input to the preparation of the statement of changes in equity. The capital or equity determined in the statement of changes in equity is fed into the equity section of the statement of financial position.

In chapter 2, we said that the statement shows the value or worth of the entity in that we subtract any liabilities from the assets of the entity to reveal the actual value of the entity.

The format and presentation is as shown in the example that follows;

JACOB SMALL REPAIRS
STATEMENT OF FINANCIAL POSITION
AS AT 31ST DECEMBER 2009

ASSETS

Non-current assets		800 000
Land and buildings		360 000
Shop equipment		280 000
Delivery vehicle		160 000
Current assets		670 000
Inventories		310 000
Debtors		240 000
Cash at bank		120 000
Total assets		**1 470 000**

EQUITY AND LIABILITIES

Capital		840 000
Paid in capital and retained earnings from previous year		758 000
Profit for the current year		82 000
Liabilities		630 000
Non-current liabilities		240 000
Mortgage loan on land and buildings		240 000
Current liabilities		390 000
Trade creditors		390 000
Total equity and liabilities		**1 470 000**

Statement of profit or loss and other comprehensive income

This statement is also primarily prepared for external users of financial information. It is made up of the other two elements of financial statements from the bottom two squares, namely the income and expenses accumulated over the reporting period.

The difference between the income and expenses for the period gives rise to either a profit if the income was higher than expenses or a loss in the event that expenses were higher than the income they helped generate.

An example of this statement is shown next;

INCOME STATEMENT
For the Years Ending December 31, 2017

REVENUES:

Sales Revenue	$500,000
Other Revenue	$0
(Less Sales Returns & Allowances	0
TOTAL REVENUES	**$500,000**
Cost of Goods Sold	150,000
GROSS PROFIT	**$350,000**

EXPENSES:

Accounting	$2,500
Advertising	25,000
Amortization	0
Bad Debt	1,000
Depreciation	50,000
Employee Payroll Tax	15,000
Employee Wages	100,000
Entertainment	0
Insurance	2,000
Interest Expense	12,000
Miscellaneous	5,000
Rent	24,000
Software	0
Telephone	2,500
Utilities	7,000
Web Hosting	500
Vehicle Expense	12,000
-	0
-	0
-	0
-	0
TOTAL EXPENSES	**$258,500**
NET INCOME BEFORE TAXES	**$91,500**
Less Income Tax Expense	0
NET INCOME	**$91,500**

Statement of changes in equity

The statement of changes in equity shows the effect of any changes that may have taken place during the reporting period. We said earlier that income or profits increase equity while expenses or losses decrease equity.

This means that equity of the entity changes, going up and down, as transactions take place and get recorded. It is the aggregate of the effect of such movements that is summarized and included in the calculation of equity at the end of the financial year of the entity.

It is the simplest report to prepare and present as it has just a few lines. It shows the balance of equity at the beginning and at the end of the reporting period and explains why equity has either grown or reduced over the reporting period.

The changes will result from profit or loss from the income statement for the year and if or not there were any drawings by the owners of the business.

Here is how the statement looks like;

KUMALO SERVICES

STATEMENT OF CHANGES IN EQUITY

FOR THE YEAR ENDED 31 DECEMBER 2002

Balance at 1 January 2002	87 750
Profit for the year	88 000
	175 750
Drawings by owner	(74 750)
Balance at 31 January 2002	101 000

Statement of cash flows

We indicated earlier that credit sales and credit purchases are also included in the income and expenses that get reported in the income statement. This does not apply to the statement of cash flows. The statement of cash flows excludes all non-cash transactions from calculation that determine the cash available at the end of the financial year.

The statement is divided into three sections the first of which shows cash flows that emanate from operating activities. The second and third sections show cash flows from investing activities as well as financing activities, respectively.

- *Investment activities* are those activities which relate to the acquisition or disposal of long term assets and investments which are not included in cash equivalents.

- *Financing activities* include in general the cash results of transactions and other events which impact on long term liabilities and owners' equity, in other words those activities which result in changes in the magnitude and composition of the debt and capital funding of the entity.

- *Operating activities* include all transactions and other events which are not investment and financing activities. These are thus the most important income generating operations of the entity. Note that the closing balance shown in this statement is always going to be the same as the bank balance given in the statement of financial position.

An example of this statement follows;

BRUMA LIMITED CASH FLOW STATEMENT FOR THE YEAR ENDED 31 DECEMBER 2007	
Cash flow from operating activities	
Net profit before taxation	45 500
Adjusted for:	
Depreciation	39 000
Loss on sale of fixed assets	1 000
Profit on sale of fixed assets	(5 000)
Investment income	(5 000)
Finance chargers	6 000
Operating profit before changes in working capital	81 500
Decrease in inventory	2 000
Increase in accounts receivable	(15 000)
Decrease in accounts payable	(10 000)
Cash generated by operations	58 500
Finance charges: Interest paid	(6 000)
Investment income: Income received	5 000
Taxation paid	(2 000)
Dividends paid	(1 000)
Net cash flow from operating activities	54 500
Cash flow from investment activities	(219 000)
Acquisition of fixed assets	(206 000)
Proceeds from the disposal of fixed assets	37 000
Investments acquired	(50 000)
Cash flow from financing activities	180 000
Proceeds from share issue	120 000
Proceeds from debenture issue	60 000
Net increase in cash and cash equivalents	15 500
Cash and cash equivalents at start of the year	15 000
Cash and cash equivalents at end of the year	R30 500

Accounting policies and notes to the accounts

In addition to the four statements explained above, the entity is also expected to disclose their accounting policies that govern how financial decisions are made in addition to the notes explaining how the numbers in the statements have been arrived at.

In the notes to the financial statements additional information, where necessary, is provided on the items that appear in the financial statements. The notes are cross-referenced to related items in the financial statements and presented systematically. The notes are usually presented in the following sequence; x The fact that the financial statements comply with IFRS x A description of the bases of measurement used in the preparation of the financial statements x A description of each accounting policy in order to have a proper understanding of the financial statements x Additional and supporting information required by applicable statement of GAAP, GRAP or IFRS.

Chapter 4

TIME VALUE OF MONEY

The concept of time value of money

Time value of money is premised on the appreciation that an amount of money today is not the same as the same amount at a particular time in the future. A $1 today is not the same as a $1 in a year's time. It is argued that an amount of money given to you today could be invested and earn interest than if the same was given to you sometime in the future, in a year's time for example.

The timing of the future cash flows is critical to the financial decisions that you make today as it has an impact on the future values of the cash flows.

Finance decisions resulting in future cash flows need to consider the implications of these differences in value.

The assessment of such future cash flows may be viewed from the future value or present value. However, the results will remain the same regardless of the viewpoint taken.

Future value

Future value calculations take a present value amount and estimate what the value will be at a certain future date. Future value measures the value at the end of the period in question. An interest rate is used to determine the extent of the loss in value. Because of the assumed loss in value, the future value is less than the present value. This implies that the present value will have to be discounted by the interest rate in order to determine its future value.

For example, the future value of a $1,000 today could be $825 or any other lesser amount depending on the rate of interest used to do the calculation of the loss in value as well as the time from now to the future date.

Present value

Present value is the other view of looking at the differences in value of cash flows. Present value looks at cash flows from the futuristic perspective to determine the value of the future amount in today's terms. Inevitably, the present value of a future amount will be lower because the future value you calculate from will be assumed to have reduced in value.

Interest calculations

Simple interest

Investopedia defines simple interest as follows;

> **"Simple interest** is a quick method of calculating the **interest** charge on a loan. **Simple interest** is determined by multiplying the daily **interest** rate by the principal by the number of days that elapse between payments".

Source:

https://www.investopedia.com/terms/s/simple_interest.asp

For example, if you invest $2,000 in a deposit account at 10% interest per annum, and held for one year, simple interest would be $200 (calculated as 2,000x10%).

Compound interest

Interest is compounded when the interest calculated is added to the principal amount and included when interest for the subsequent period is calculated. Effectively, the interest that is quoted is not exactly the same as the actual interest that is achieved or paid as a result of this incremental effect.

Here is an example.

You borrow a $2,000 at 10% for a two year period with interest being compounded annually.

Compound interest would be calculated as follows;
Interest at the end of the first year is 2,000x10% = 200. Before interest for the second year is calculated, the 200 is first added to the principal amount of 2,000. Thus interest at the end of the second year is 2,200 x 10% = 220.

Simple interest vs compound interest

Simple interest

Period	Principal Amount	Interest Rate	Interest Amount
End of first year	2,000	10%	200
End of second year	2,000	10%	200
Total interest in the two year period			**400**

Compound interest

Period	Principal Amount	Interest Rate	Interest Amount
End of first year	2,000	10%	200
End of second year	2,200	10%	220
Total interest in the two year period			**420**

As can be seen in the above two examples, compound interest increases the cost if you are borrowing for a longer period while you would be beneficial if you were investing in a fixed deposit account for example since you would earn more value for your investment.

An understanding of compound interest is important when making finance decisions because the cost of borrowing and the rate at which future cash flows are discounted will impact the ultimate net cash flows.

Compounding more than once per year

The calculation of compound interest in the examples above has been on the assumption that compounding takes place once in a year. However, in real life, and more often than not, the period of compounding is less than a year; monthly, quarterly, half yearly or even daily.

It is imperative, therefore, that the interest rate gets adjusted in order to account for the different time periods that may apply.

An example will help make this clearer. Using the $2,000 example above. Let us now say that interest is compounded quarterly or half yearly.

The interest calculated will be as follows;

Interest compounded annually (as calculated above)

Year	Period	Principal Amount	Interest Rate p.a.	Interest Amount
Year 1		2,000	10%	200
Year 2		2,200	10%	220
Total interest in the two year period				**420**

Interest compounded semi-annually

Year	Period	Principal Amount	Interest Rate p.a.	Interest Amount
Year 1	1st half	2,000	5.00%	100
Year 1	2nd half	2,100	5.00%	105
Year 2	1st half	2,205	5.00%	110
Year 2	2nd half	2,315	5.00%	116
Total interest in the two year period				**431**

Interest compounded quarterly

Year	Period	Principal Amount	Interest Rate p.a.	Interest Amount
Year 1	1st half	2,000	2.50%	50
Year 1	2nd half	2,050	2.50%	51
Year 1	1st half	2,101	2.50%	53
Year 1	2nd half	2,154	2.50%	54
Year 2	1st half	2,208	2.50%	55
Year 2	2nd half	2,263	2.50%	57
Year 2	1st half	2,319	2.50%	58
Year 2	2nd half	2,377	2.50%	59
Total interest in the two year period				**437**

When interest is compounded semi-annually, notice that the annual interest of 10% is divided by two. This is because the interest is compounded twice in the year so only half (5%) applies to each half of the year.

Similarly, when interest is compounded quarterly, the annual rate of 10% is divided by 4 to take the frequency into account.

It is clear from the above three calculations that the interest amount for the three different compounding periods differs. The principle will also apply when compounding takes place monthly.

This is important for financial decision makers to bear in mind as the cost of borrowing will be different dependent on the frequency of compounding.

Time value of money and decision making

There are various financial decisions that need to be made in relation to time value of money. We will look at two of them; investment decisions and finance decisions to highlight the relationship with the time value of money concept.

Investment decisions

Long-term investment decisions usually require large amounts of capital. They involve choosing from available options each of which must be assessed and realistic cash flow estimates calculated. Particular attention must be paid to such decisions as erroneous or ill-informed decisions could result in huge losses being incurred.

Financing decisions

Financing decisions have to do with the sources of funding to enable your entity to do what needs to be done. It is necessary to consider the cost of such sources so that you can compare with the future inflows to determine if a particular project will yield benefits to the entity or not.

Chapter 5

CAPITAL BUDGETING TECHNIQUES

Capital budgeting techniques are used to help financial decision makers assess options by comparing out flows of funds with inflows in order to determine the viability of the investment. The techniques that are used to achieve this could be non-discounted or discounted techniques. We will look at some techniques in each category.

Non- discounted cash flow techniques

Non-discounted techniques do not take time value of money into account when assessing projects or investment options. Two such techniques are the Accounting Rate of Return (the ARR) and the Pay-Back-Period (PBP).

- *ARR*

The ARR uses accounting profits to assess capital investments. It is calculated by taking after tax average profits from accounting and dividing them by the average investment. The advantage of this method is that it uses actual accounting profits.

$$ARR = \frac{\text{average profits after tax}}{\text{Average investment}}$$

When comparing two projects for instance, the project or investment option with a higher ARR should be preferred to one which has a lower ARR.

An example (adapted from Correia et al) showing how to calculate the ARR is given next.

The following facts relate to Project R. The cost of the project is $1.1. It is expected to have a residual value of zero in five years' time. The cash flows for each year are depicted in the following table. The project is depreciated at 20% straight line per year for accounting purposes, and this also reflects the depreciation deduction used for tax purposes. Assume a 28% tax

Project R	0	1	2	3	4	5
Cost	- 1 100 000					
Cashflows		300 000	450 000	450 000	450 000	450 000
Depreciation		- 220 000	- 220 000	- 220 000	- 220 000	- 220 000
Net income	- 1 100 000	80 000	230 000	230 000	230 000	230 000
Taxation at 28%		- 22 400	- 64 400	- 64 400	- 64 400	- 64 400
Net income after tax	- 1 100 000	57 600	165 600	165 600	165 600	165 600
Net book value	1 100 000	880 000	660 000	440 000	220 000	-

Average net income

$(57,600 + 165,600 + 165,600 + 165,600 + 165,600)/5 = 144,000$

Average investment

$(1,100,000 - 0)/2 = 550,000$

$$ARR = \frac{144,000}{550,000} \times 100$$

Notes

1 The cash flows for each year are given s given in the question
2 Depreciation is found by dividing the 1,100,000 investment divided by the 5 year project life
3 Taxation is calculated at 28% of net income

4   Net book value is cost less accumulated depreciation
       1,100,000 less 220,000 depreciation each year

5   Average investment = Initial cost - zero residual value divided
       by 2

- **PBP**

Investopedia defines PBP as follows;

"The payback period is the length of time required to recover the cost of an investment. The payback period of a given investment or project is an important determinant of whether to undertake the position or project, as longer payback periods are typically not desirable for investment positions".

Source: Payback Period

https://www.investopedia.com/terms/p/paybackperiod.asp#ixzz5 MMDZZd5k

Example

A company needs to decide between investing Project A or Project B. It is company policy to opt for the project that gives the shortest payback period.

The investment and cash flows associated with both projects are given as follows;

	Year	Project A	Project B
Investment	0	- 12 000	- 12 000
Cash flows	1	4 000	2 000
	2	6 000	4 000
	3	6 000	4 000
	4	-	8 000

Which project should the company invest in?

The PBP for Project A is 2 years and 4 months. The 4 months is found by taking the (2,000) of the investment still remaining to be recovered and dividing it by the available 6,000 cash inflow and then multiplying by 12 months to convert the answer into months.

	-	12 000	
Year 1		4 000	
	-	8 000	Investment still to be recovered
Year 2		6 000	
	-	2 000	Investment still to be recovered
Year 3		6 000	

The PBP for Project B is 3 years and 3 months calculated in the same way as we did for Project A.

	-	12 000	
Year 1		2 000	
	-	10 000	Investment still to be recovered
Year 2		4 000	
	-	6 000	Investment still to be recovered
Year 3		4 000	
	-	2 000	Investment still to be recovered
Year 4		8 000	

In this example, Project A would be preferred because it has a shorter PBP than Project B.

The two disadvantages of this technique are that it does not take into account the time value of money and ignores the cash flows that occur after the payback period.

Discounted cashflow techniques

The common discounted cash flow techniques include the Net Present Value (NPV) and the Internal Rate of Return (IRR)

- ### *NPV*

The NPV is the present value of cash inflows less the initial investment. It reflects the amount of income that the project will produce at a pre-determined rate of return. It is calculated by subtracting the project's initial investment from the present value of the project's cash inflows, discounted at a rate equal to, for example, the firm's cost of capital.

NPV, because it takes into account the time value of money, is considered a more sophisticated capital budgeting technique than the payback method. If the NPV is greater than 0, the firm will earn a return greater than its cost of capital (because the cost of capital is the discount rate used to find NPV). If more than one project is being assessed and they all have NPVs greater than zero, the project with the highest NPV will be selected.

Example

A project costs $100,000 with a zero residual value after its 3-year lifespan. Cash inflows are expected to be $48,000 in the first year, $55,000 in the second year and $63,000 in the final year. The cost of capital for this company is 14%. Compute the NPV for the project and advise management if they should invest in it.

There are a number of ways to calculate the NPV, the easiest of which would be using a financial calculator. You could also use a computer spreadsheet, financial tables or a mathematical formula. We will use the financial table method to demonstrate the decision making process.

	Cashflow	PV Factor	Present Value
Cost	(100,000)	1.0000	(100,000)
Year 1	48,000	0.8772	42,106
Year 2	55,000	0.7695	42,323
Year 3	63,000	0.6750	42,525
		NPV	26,953

This project could be undertaken because it has a positive NPV. The NPV is greater than zero which indicates that the present value of the inflows at the 14% interest rate is greater than the initial investment.

• *IRR*

Unlike the NPV method that provides a financial amount, the IRR determines the rate of return that equates to the investment opportunity of $0 (the present value of cash flows equals the initial investment). It is the compound annual rate of return that the firm will earn if it invests in the project and receives the value of IRR.

Example

Using the same cash flow information from the example on the NPV above, we now wish to calculate the IRR for this project.

We can use an HP10bII Financial calculator to determine the IRR is 30.28%. You will have to learn how to use a financial calculator to find the IRR. Take note that there are slight differences in the process to be followed when you use other brands of financial calculators. You need to follow the specific steps as given in the financial calculator that you use.

NPV or ARR?

Usually, the results from the NPV and IRR calculations will point in the same direction in terms of which project to invest in. But there are times when the two techniques will result in different answers. In such a case, you should take the NPV because the NPV calculates the present value of each cashflow separately using progressively different rates whereas the IR uses the same rate for all the cash flows.

Chapter 6

ANALYSIS AND INTERPRETATION OF FINANCIAL STATEMENTS

Earlier, we saw how financial statements are used to convey information, regarding the financial position and performance of an entity, to the different users of this information. In this chapter, we will be looking at analysing financial statements.

While financial statements provide useful information on the health and performance of an entity, in and of themselves, they have some limitations. For example, the difficulty of comparing one balance sheet to another. Let's say that one firm has made a profit of $100 million in a particular year and another firm makes $250,000 in the same period.

On the face of it, it is not easy to tell which of these two firms has performed better than the other. It could be that the $100 million profit for the one firm represents only 5% of the sales while that of the other firm could well be 46%. Clearly, the $250,000 profit firm has recorded a higher return in this period than the other firm even though the Dollar amount is much smaller.

You can see from this illustration that converting the profit as a percentage of sales brings both firms to the same level of measurement. That is the major benefit derived from ratio analysis. Ratio analysis is the most commonly used tool to analyse financial statements.

The statement of financial position (balance sheet) and the statement of income are the two sources of information that is needed to analyse financial statements.

Ratio analysis is divided into different categories, each measuring a different aspect of the finances of the firm. Some ratios measure the profitability of the entity. You also have liquidity ratios, activity or efficiency ratios and debt ratios. In addition, there are a few other ratios, but we will not include them here. There are several ratios within each of these categories.

Profitability ratios

Let's start with the profitability ratios that measure the percentage of profit that you make in every dollar of sales. With all the profitability ratios, the higher it is, the better.

The ratios that we will discuss here include the following;

- Gross profit margin
- Net profit margin
- Return on investment (return on assets)
- Return on equity
- Earnings per share (EPS).

Gross profit margin or gross profit ratio measures how much gross profit you make in every dollar of sale. Is it 5%, 10%, 20% or whatever the case may. The way to calculate the gross profit margin is to first divide the gross profit by sales and then multiplying by 100 in order to convert it into a percentage.

Gross Profit Margin = $\dfrac{\text{Gros profit}}{\text{Sales}} \times 100$

Net profit margin which is the profit after removing all expenses and after paying preference share dividend. NPM expresses the net profit as a percentage of sales. It is arrived at by dividing the net profit by sales and then multiplying by 100 to obtain the ratio in percentage terms.

Net Profit Margin = $\dfrac{\text{Operating profit}}{\text{Sales}} \times 100$

Return on Assets (ROA), also called *Return on Investment (ROI).* This ratio measures the overall efficiency of management in using available assets to generate profit. It is found by dividing the profit after subtracting preference share dividend by total assets. It is also expressed as a percentage.

ROA = $\dfrac{\text{Profit} - \text{Preference Share Dividend}}{\text{Total Assets}} \times 100$

Return on equity measures the return that owners have earned on their investment. The higher the rate, the better. It is calculated by dividing the net profit after tax by the shareholders equity and expressed as a percentage.

ROE = $\dfrac{\text{Net profit after tax}}{\text{Shareholders' equity}} \times 100$

Next you have *Earnings Per Share* or *EPS*. EPS is also a profitability ratio. It is of interest to people who have shares within a particular entity. It indicates the number of dollars that each ordinary share has earned during a period. To calculate it, you take the profit for the year, less preference dividends and then divide this by the number of ordinary shareholder shares that have been issued.

$$EPS = \frac{Net\ profit - preference\ dividend}{Number\ of\ ordinary\ shares\ in\ issue}$$

Liquidity ratios

Liquidity ratios measure the liquidity (cash or near cash) available to a business to meet short term obligations as they fall due. Liquidity ratios include the current ratio and the quick ratio, also called the acid test ratio.

Current ratio

Arrived at by diving current assets by current liabilities, this ratio measures your ability as a business, to pay your short-term commitments (current liabilities) as they fall due using available current assets. The higher this ratio is, the better.

$$Current\ ratio = \frac{Current\ assets}{Current\ liabilities}$$

Quick ratio (Acid test ratio)

The quick ratio is like the current ratio we just discussed. The difference is that you deduct the inventory from the current assets before dividing by the current liabilities. The rationale behind this is that it would be misleading to check your liquidity accurately if you include inventory in the current assets balance as the inventory may not sell as quickly as you would like, and therefore cannot be treated as being available to be used to meet short term liabilities.

$$\text{Current ratio} = \frac{\text{Current assets - inventory}}{\text{Current liabilities}}$$

Net working capital

Even though not strictly a ratio, NWC is arrived at after deducting your current liabilities from current assets. The resultant figure represents what is available for a business to implement whatever operations it has planned.

$$\text{NWC} = \text{Current assets -current liabilities}$$

Activity ratios

These ratios measure the efficiency with which different accounts are converted into sales or cash or into inflows or outflows depending on the specific ratio that you're looking. In this category, we will discuss three ratios; namely the inventory turnover ratio, average collection period and the average payments period.

Inventory turnover

The inventory turnover ratio measures the number of times that a business can sell or to turn over the inventory in a year. It is arrived at by taking the cost of goods sold and dividing it by inventory. It is expressed as the number of times inventory has been turned over in the reporting period. Clearly, the higher the ratio, the better for the business.

$$\text{Inventory turnover} = \frac{\text{Cost of sales}}{\text{Inventory}}$$

Average collection period

This ratio measures how long (on average) it takes you as a business to collect cash after making a credit sale. The shorter this period is the better for you. It is calculated as follows;

$$\text{Average collection period} = \frac{\text{Accounts receivable}}{\text{Annual sales}} \times 365$$

The average collection period is denoted in number of days. Note that 360 is sometimes used to convert the answer into the number of days in a year instead of the calendar 365 days.

Average payment period is on the opposite end of the average collection period. It measures (on average) how many days it takes you as a business to pay off your credit purchases. The formula is as follows;

$$\text{Average payment period} = \frac{\text{Trade and other payables}}{\text{Annual purchases}} \times 365$$

Ideally, your average collection period should be shorter than the average payment period, otherwise, you would have to look for cash elsewhere to pay your liabilities while still waiting to collect cash from your credit sales.

Total asset turnover

This ratio measures the efficiency with which you use your assets in order to generate sales. The higher the ratio, the better for the business.

$$\text{Total asset turnover} = \frac{\text{Annual Sales}}{\text{Total assets}}$$

Debt (solvency) ratios

In this category, we will discuss only two ratios; the debt ratio and the debt to equity ratio. Debt ratios speak to the amount of debt that you have used to finance your assets. The greater this ratio is, the greater the amount of borrowed funds that the business has used to finance its assets.

Debt ratio

When you divide the total liabilities by total assets and multiply by a 100 to convert the answer into a percentage, you get the debt ratio. This ratio tells you what proportion of your assets have been financed using borrowed money. A higher ratio shows that a larger portion of your assets are financed by borrowed funds. This indicates a greater risk for the business.

$$\text{Debt ratio} = \frac{\text{Total liabilities}}{\text{Total assets}}$$

Debt to equity ratio

The debt to equity ratio indicates the relationship between long term debt provided by creditors and the funds provided by the owners of the firm. This is expressed as a percentage and shows the portion of long-term liabilities as a percentage of owners' equity.

$$\text{Debt} - \text{equity ratio} = \frac{\text{Long-term debt}}{\text{Shareholders' equity}} \times 100$$

Conclusion

Caution must be exercised to ensure that decisions are not made based only on one ratio. It is always advisable to calculate several ratios and interpret them as a whole before making decisions as this gives a more balanced view of the financial health, or otherwise, of a firm.

References

1. Correia, C., Flynn, D., Uliana, E. and Wormald, M. (2013). Financial Management. 7th ed. Cape Town, Juta.

2. Gitman, L. J., Smith, M. B., Hall, J., Lowies, B., Marx, J., Strydom, B. and van de Merwe, A. (2010). Principles of Managerial Finance – Global and Southern African Perspectives. Cape Town, Pearson Education.

3. Marx, J., De Swardt, C. and Nortje, A. (2003). Financial Management in Southern Africa. Cape Town, Pearson Education.

ABOUT THE AUTHOR

"As an experienced, astute and versa-tile training consultant and executive coach with international experience, I help my clients develop several soft skills courses and facilitate training effectively in various subjects"

Claude has been involved in training, coaching and consulting for more than 10 years. He is the founder and Chief Executive Officer of Mapalo Management Services, He is a well-travelled professional, having lived in three different countries and visited nearly all the countries in the Central, Eastern and Southern African countries. He is a widely exposed professional who has great interpersonal and intercultural experience and skills.

He has spoken and presented papers at some international conferences/symposia on human resource management, motivation and leadership in general.